DOG HC

HOW TO BUILD A DOG HOUSE IN LESS THAN 30 DAYS

By Beverly Hill

Introduction

I want to thank you and congratulate you for choosing the book, *"DOG HOUSE PLAN: HOW TO BUILD A DOG HOUSE IN LESS THAN 30 DAYS"*.

This book contains proven steps and strategies on how to build a wonderful dog house for your pet.

One of the closet pet and domestic animal that is found around man is the Dog. Dogs are loved by men and women, children and youth in most cases, and nearly all the families around the world had once upon a time had a dog within their house and premises. Domestic Dogs play important roles as animals within the confinement of the home and it is not surprising that there has been legislation on how to keep and maintain a dog in any house or neighborhood.

We have also witnessed so many areas where dogs are used as security means for searching, keeping vigilance and hunting to mention a few. Contained in this book is extensive information on how to construct a dog house in less than 30 days and so much more information that you may be unaware of.

Thanks again for choosing this book, I hope you enjoy it!

ABOUT THE AUTHOR

Beverly Hill is a sociologist. She is the CEO of C.E.F Associates and formerly served as head of department of sociology in Premier Natural Resources Inc.

A graduate of Nelson High School also graduated from the University of Toronto with a B.A in economics and finance and holds an M.S from Cambridge University in public relations and PhD in sociology.

She has written many articles on human equality, animal rights, environmental issues, personal development and peace keeping in different newspapers. She has also appeared in many magazines and is frequently interviewed for articles on family, race, socioeconomic status, and how to survive in your environment. She has also worked on the importance of health of relationship between parents and children. Her book 'The Middle Child' focuses on the importance of the attention given to the children and what to expect from them. This book helps parents understand their children.

In addition to these works she is also the author of 'Surviving Alone ' which is about her own childhood growing up; she writes about her family struggles living on a low income budget and growing her own food to survive.

C.E.F Associates formed in 1999 in Idaho, USA she worked both nationally and internationally. This is a consulting company which has clients all over the world. Ms. Hill the CEO of the company is the main reason of the huge client base because of her servings in foreign countries.

TABLE OF CONTENT

Chapter 1

THE ROLE OF DOGS

The role of dogs in society cannot be over emphasized as there are issues to be uncovered that concerns dogs. Hence, there are a variety of species of dogs in the world today. Scientist and biologist have done amazing research and have been able to create ground breaking discoveries about dogs. The subject on dogs is so wide, this book will discuss additional information on other topics about dogs. But before we forge ahead with building a dog house, lets us highlight a few points about what we need to know about dogs in general.

What is a Dog? A dog is a highly variable domestic mammal (Canis familiaris) closely related to the common wolf (canis lupus) and there are various species of dogs available in the world today each with natural strength and conditions, especially the different types that can be trained by human to adapt to certain circumstances to become useful in many areas such as security, entertainment and detection of crimes or hunting etc.

Some of the common species of dogs are the English cocker spaniel which is a breed of spaniels that have square muzzles, wide well developed noses, and distinctive heads which are ideally half muzzle and half skull with the forehead and skull arched and slightly flattened,

The Alsatian dogs is a very good species makes good security dogs a highly developed canines that can be trained to hunt down criminals, the blood hound dogs is also one of the very best dogs that has highly developed abilities when trained to assist in crime detection and hunting for clues that can lead to detecting and helping catch criminals. Also it is a good dog that can be used for hunting purposes. The list goes on, as there are many varieties and breads available all over the world today.

Chapter 2

THE TWO MAJOR CATEGORIES OF DOGS

There are two categories of dogs in the world today, (1) domestic dogs and (2) Wild dogs

Domestic Dogs

Domestic dogs are the species of dogs that can be tolerated by human beings and can also be kept at home. Domestic dogs constitute as the wonderful pet any family can have in their homes. It can be a little puppy to the larger and bigger kind of dog. Both young and old are always enchanted by the domestic dogs and they serve wonderful purposes in your homes. One thing that is predominantly common among domestic dogs is they have the natural and great ability to recognize its owners and other members of the family that lives in the same household or neighborhood of its owners.

Secondly, when the domestic dogs see someone like its master or a member of the family where the dogs is resident in, they will shake its tail to signify that he is happy to see its master or family members. The domestic dogs most of the time are playful and delightful and loves to be caress with much love.

The domestic dog often times is not keen to see strange faces around the house, and that is why they will always bark at strangers, simply because the domestic dog is not familiar with the strange face. Sometimes, a dog that is a bigger size, if it's free and not chained can attack a stranger with the probability of inflecting injuries, because the dog is not familiar with strangers. This is also a way of creating security awareness or consciousness among residents of the house when the dog barks; it is demonstrating and alerting the members of the house or neighborhood that there is an intruder.

Some domestic dogs have the tendency to be able to understand signs and some will respond to it if well trained. We have seen how a tamed dog can run some common task around the home, which sometimes causes amazement to some people who have not had any dog in their house.

Wild Dogs

Wild dogs are of different species, they are non-domestic. That is, they cannot be said to be successfully kept at home as pets. They are dangerous and many of them are carnivorous animals who feed on flesh except hyena which feeds on other death carcasses of other animals and are further classified according to their mode of feeding as scavengers. The wild dog family comprises of wolfs, fox, hyena etc.

Now, these categories of dogs cannot be kept as pets, they are usually kept in zoos or tamed and used in circus or sports entertainment. Many countries promulgate laws that will allow these categories of dogs to be kept in game reserve, which is a habitat for preserving and preventing wild lives from being hunted into extinction.

Chapter 3

USES OF DOGS

AS PETS

Domestic Dogs are kept as pets and a lot of people and families love to keep pets just for the fun of it. Besides, they are often good company to keep because of its ability to draw attentions to neighbors in time of emergency or when there is trouble around the house.

Security Purposes

Dogs are used as security dogs by the Police and private security companies. They also make use of dogs to assist in detecting crimes and give clues to track the foot prints of a fugitive. Considering the current waves of criminal activities, security dogs can render effective services in detecting crime easily.

The benefits of the domestic dogs are immeasurable, but one thing is having a domestic dog and another thing is having a good house to keep it in. We are talking about having a wonderful dog house for your lovely dog which you either keep as a pet or you are keeping it for security. If you are thinking of building a dog house, you will need a suitable one to keep your dog safe and happy.

There are many dog houses designs and construction beginning from the simple ones to the most complex form of house construction for your dogs. What we are going to demonstrate is how to build a dog house in less than 30 days that will keep you happy and you will be proud of your efforts and what you have done. So sit tight and read and secure the necessary knowledge that you need to build a wonderful house for your lovingly dog.

Sporting Activities

Dog race is one of the famous outdoor sporting activities where dogs are used in sports racing and some people will bet money on the dogs during the race. Also, a dog can help in a fox chase. This is a sport the dog and the master can enjoy together.

How to build a dog house in less than 30 days

After obtaining your dog, you may want to build a house for your dog. It is not enough to just have a house you need to have the knowledge about the various things that is needed in order to keep the house neat and tidy. You don't want to have a dog house with bad orders. Let's take a look at the procedure to build a nice dog house for your beautiful pet.

Chapter 4

MATERIALS REQUIRED FOR BUILDING A DOG HOUSE

The materials you will need to help build a dog house are not expensive and can be easily purchase from a nearby store. Take a look at the list of materials you will need for the construction of your dog house.

Tools Required: Sawhorses, drill with screw-driving attachment, miter saw, 1-3/8-inch spade bit with spur cutters, hand stapler, brush, medium-grit sandpaper, orbital sander, utility knife with regular and single-cutting hook blades, assorted drill bits and countersink bit, hammer, circular saw with plywood-cutting blade, framing square, clamps, jig saw with cross-cut blade.

The materials you will need to construct the dog house are listed below:

Roofing cement

15-lb. asphalt-impregnated felt roofing paper

¾" sheet of exterior-grade plywood (not pressure-treated)

1 bundle (or about 12) 2-tab asphalt shingles

3/8" galvanized staples

2x2x6' fir or cedar board

2x4x8' pressure-treated board

1-1/4" galvanized wood screws

Low-VOC paint or stain

3" galvanized wood screws

¾" galvanized roofing nails

NOTE: Sometimes dogs spent most of their time outdoors. This design will help you construct a unique dog house from a single piece or sheet of plywood and few pieces of lumber. The dog house should be design to provide accommodations for the type and size of the dog that you have. Large dog house is not necessary, simply because dogs have the tendency to feel more secure in little spaces. Also, dogs usually prefer a small space with little opening to help heat them during the cold weather.

Hence, the design is for a small sized dog, up to an estimation of fifty pounds. The exterior grade plywood will be good enough, while you cut about ¾ inches-thick from the sheets to make the dog house. The reasons we are using this type of wood is because the wood serves as a natural insulator which enables and keeps the dog house cool in the summer and warm during the winter months.

It is advisable to always make use of the woods that are free of splinters for the safety of your dog. It is recommended using pressure treated wood only for the base of the dog house where your dog cannot chew on it. Pressure treated woods are designed with chemicals that could adversely affect your dog. Painting of the dog house should be done with VOC finishes.

Chapter 5

PROCEDURES TO BUILD A DOG HOUSE

Make a sketch of the design of the dog house

Step 1

Make the following cut list

2x4 into four pieces for the construction of the base floor

2 at 22-1/2 inches length

2 at 23 inches length

2x2 fir or cedar into eight pieces for the framing part of the building

4 corner framing (i.e.) 13 inches long

Use the straightedge and framing square to construct as shown in the diagram on the sheet of plywood using the above dimensions. The door way should be an estimated 10 inches wide and 13 inches in height.

Allow 3 inches in height of lip at the base of the hole to shield the base and the panel's lower base. The door opening for the dog should be made at about ¾ of the height of the dog.

Remember dogs like little space to protect them during winter and they need the feeling of warmness so don't make the door opening for the dog to big, just a little cozy inn so the dog can always sneak in and out will be great.

Step Two

Make the drawings on the plywood and cut the splinter, making sure that all the cuts fit in properly as indicated in the above figure. Make sure you follow the dimensions as presented above during your cutting to make sure the woods fit the prescribed sizes.

Also, when cutting the roof panel with the blade, remember to set it at an angle of 45 degree. This will ensure a tight fitting at the roof with the appropriate dimension. Make sure you are careful with the blades during the cut.

Cut the roof panel at a wider surface with 20 inches dimension as shown in the above diagram.

Jig saw is to be used in cutting the plywood to bring out the doorway. Drill 3/8 inch diameter hole for the jig saw blade at each base side of the entrance by following the lines and do the final cut out.

Make sure you drill few holes in the back panel to allow for cross ventilation for the dog house, to allow comfort for your dog during the hot summer weather.

After cutting out the pieces of plywood, smoothen all the edges with orbital sand paper or sanding block, also use the medium grit sand paper to remove any unsmooth spots/splinters.

Step Three

Cut the pieces for the base according to the cut list mentioned earlier by using a power miter saw or circular saw. Remember to wear your mask while doing the cutting of the treated lumber to avoid being affected. Assemble the base frame 2x4 parts.

Put the 23" pieces side of the base fixing in the 22-1/2" front and back pieces together. By using a countersink pre-drill holes and fasten the pieces cut out for the base together using 3 inches galvanized wood screws at each end.

Insert the bottom panel on the base side and flush all edges, square fasten the bottom to the base side using the 1/-1/4" galvanized wood screws and sink the screw heads just beneath the face.

Step Four

Cut the frames from the 2x2s. Gather the sides by fixing one 15 inches vertical side frames to each edge of the panels with unique flushes made at the edge of the plywood plus the top of the panel. A one space between the base of the corner frame and the bottom edge of the side should be maintained. Bring each piece of frames with 3 of the 1-1/4" galvanized wood screws fixed or driven through the plywood into the frames. Connect the panels at the base, making sure the front and back edge of the panels flushes with the front respectively. Connect the sides to the base with wood that is galvanized and screws driven at all 4-5 inches round the border.

While the side panels are fixed to the base, put the assembly at one end. Also, put the back panel into the assembled structure, causing the bottom edges of the panels to meet accordingly. Hold the back panel to the vertical framing supporting it with 1-1/4 inches wood (i.e. the galvanized wood) screws driven at 4 inches. At the bottom edge, drive the screws through the panel to the floor, but don't allow the tips of the screw to poke through the floor. Turn the dog house over and repeat the process for the front panel.

Remember! In order to make things easy for you, you do not need to do all the construction immediately. It is advisable to take it one step at a time; you will still be able to make a fantastic house in less than 30 days, so there is no need to rush it. You can work on it during your leisure time and make it a fun project.

Step Five

Fix the 13 inches frame to the other parts to the inwards edges of the rooflines as indicated in step 4 above. Making sure that the front and back panel flushes with the edges by positioning the frames half way between the top and bottom roofline. Hold the frames together with 1-1//4 inches galvanized wood with screws driven inside the plywood leading into the frame. Make sure the panels join well with the peak of the roof. Fasten the roof framings with the panels using the 1-1/4" galvanized wood screws and allow it to be fixed tightly.

Step Six

Begin roofing as indicated in above figure with 15lb of asphalt impregnated roofing paper. This will help protect the inside of your dog house by keeping the inside dry. Staple the layers with a hammer stapler using 3/8" galvanized staples. Flush with the edges of the panels by using utility knifes to adjust it.

Use galvanized nails of about ¾ inches to drive in and affixed properly without allowing any nail to protrude from the roof so it will not hurt the dog when he goes in. Repeat the process for all covering, gently press these shingles so they lay flat, you should allow the edges at the front sides to overlap the plywood by ¾ inches to enable protection from moisture.

Trim off any excess layers around the roof with a utility knife leaving out the overlapping at the edges to enable protection of plywood against moisture.

Step Seven

Finally, paint the house using a low VOC exterior painting. And before you let your dog go inside, allow the paints to thoroughly dry out to void paint odor. Check out above figure, you will see how happy your dog will be when he has its own house.

Conclusion

Thank you again for choosing this book!

I hope this book was able to help you to build your dog house.

It is an ideal and interesting thing to keep pets, and a dog having its own house is a way of hygienically maintaining a dog in the family. Dogs are wonderful animals and they also require care and better treatment, like protection during winter and summer. Above all if you keep your dog outside, make sure you also have a dog house to keep it safe. Cheers!

©AkaMissBeth Creation

Finally, if you enjoyed this book, would you be kind enough to leave a review for this book on Amazon? It'd be greatly appreciated!

Thank you and good luck!

Preview Of 'DOG TREAT RECIPES: LEARN HOW TO MAKE AWESOME TREATS FOR YOUR BEST FRIEND'

Chapter 1

DOG TREAT RECIPES

Dog lovers may want to give their pet dogs some treats to reward their god behavior. Take your pick from these various dog treat recipes.

Dog biscuit recipes include peanut butter, eggs, and flour and bone meal. Cheesy dog biscuits include cheddar cheese, chicken broth, whole wheat flour, cornmeal and oats, while bacon flavored dog treats make use of whole wheat flour, milk, eggs and bacon fat for flavor. There are also microwavable dog biscuits that use a variety of flours including cracked wheat, rye, and whole wheat.

Vegetarian treat recipes include vegetarian dog biscuits which use peanuts for the dog's protein source. Vegan dog biscuit recipes and doggie Christmas cookies also include peanut butter, honey, cornmeal, and flour.

Copper cookie cutters in fun shapes, such as big and small dog bones, cows, roosters, and squirrels will make fine dog treats that you can make into biscuit treats for your four-legged friend.

If you love baking for your dog, there are breads and cookie recipes that you can follow. These recipes include: peanut butter, bones, chicken and honey biscuits, big boy beef biscuits, and everyday biscuits. Other dog treats include parmesan herb treats, apple cinnamon drops, whole wheat cream cheese Danish, peanut butter and honey oat crunchies, and beef biscuits. It is important to invest in high quality baking sheets that have a non stick finish to come up with these treats.

BEVERLY HILL

To check out the rest of (DOG TREAT RECIPE BOOK: LEARN HOW TO MAKE AWESOME TREATS FOR YOUR BEST FRIEND) go to Amazon.com

Check Out My Other Books

Below you'll find another popular book that is on Amazon and Kindle as well. Alternatively, you can visit my author page on Amazon to see other work done by me.

DOG SEPARATION ANXIETY: LEARN HOW TO CURE YOUR DOG SEPARATION ANXIETY

You can simply search for the title on the Amazon website to find them.

Bonus: FREE BOOK

Beginners Guide to Yoga & Meditation

So many people have achieved a sense of wellness they have never felt before just through a few short yoga sessions. You can Download your **FREE BOOK** in the back of any of my eBooks

NOTES

NOTES

NOTES

NOTES

NOTES

NOTES

NOTES

NOTES

NOTES

Made in the USA
Las Vegas, NV
26 August 2022

54021034R00024